T0345909

This Shadowy Place

Poetry Books also by Dick Allen:

Present Vanishing: Poems

The Day Before: New Poems

Ode to the Cold War: Poems New and Selected

Flight and Pursuit

Overnight in the Guest House of the Mystic

Regions With No Proper Names

Anon and Various Time Machine Poems

This Shadowy Place

POEMS

Dick Allen

WINNER OF THE NEW CRITERION POETRY PRIZE

St. Augustine's Press
SOUTH BEND, IN 2014

*Funding for this year's New Criterion Poetry Prize
has been provided by Joy & Michael Millette*

www.staugustine.net

Library of Congress Cataloging-in-Publication Data:

Allen, Dick, 1939–
  [Poems. Selections]
  This Shadowy Place : Poems / Dick Allen. — 1st Edition.
    pages cm
  "Winner of the New Criterion Poetry Prize."
  ISBN 978-1-58731-859-7 (hardcover: acid-free paper)
  I. Title.
PS3551.L3922A6 2013
811'.54 – dc23   2013039872

Contents

Why is Life So Hard   *1*

I

The Book Lovers of Round Lake   *7*

Sleepy Old Towns   *8*

Stepping on Shadows   *10*

The Poet's House   *12*

The House With Only the Sound of a Dog Barking Inside   *14*

I Was Eighteen   *15*

Elvis   *16*

Winter Semester   *18*

Box Trucks   *21*

Ballade of the Protester   *23*

Because a Blue Heron Flew Overhead   *25*

II

Other Fish in the Sea   *29*

Joe's Song   *31*

Buddha's Hand   *33*

Out of the Blue   *34*

Do You Know the Muffin Man?   *35*

The Beginner   *37*

Turning Over a New Leaf   *39*

The Folk Ballad of Neil Armstrong 40

Bronx Catholic 43

Cavalry 44

III

A Touch of Strange 49

Prayer Flags 51

Political Styles 53

Tiananmen Square 54

In This Time of Disbelief 56

Quagmire 59

Pitfalls 60

In the Closed School, In the Occupied Country 61

France 62

Teaching the Logical Fallacy 63

Mare's Nest 65

Putting Legs on a Snake 67

The Cause 68

IV

Russet 71

Triolet for Stephen Hawkings 72

At 65 73

The Watershed	*76*
Quantum Physicists in a Night Garden	*78*
Wild Oats	*79*
Sudden Death	*80*
Cloud No Bigger than a Man's Hand	*81*
Solace	*82*

To Lincoln Anton Allen Weir

May this book be a valediction for your new century or, at the very least, a blessing.

Acknowledgments

Grateful Acknowledgement is made to the editors and publishers of the following, in which some of these poems first appeared, a few in slightly different form: *Agni Online, American Poetry Monthly, Atlantic Monthly, Baltimore Review, Boulevard, Caduceus, The Cape Rock, Cincinnati Review, Edge City Review, The Formalist, Free Lunch, Gettysburg Review, Hampden-Sydney Poetry Review, Hudson Review, Iambs & Trochees, Image, Margie, Massachusetts Review, Measure, Nassau Review, Ontario Review, Pivot, New England Review, Only the Sea Keeps: Poetry of the Tsunami, Poetry, Raintown Review, The Random House Book of Light Verse, The New Criterion, Urbanus.*

"The Beginner" was reprinted in *Verse Daily*.

"Solace" has been set to music by William Bolcom. This composition is available for performances without cost from Edward B. Marks Music Company, 126 East 38th Street, New York, NY 10016.

This Shadowy Place

Why Is Life so Hard?

Because rocks are hard, and diamonds,
and hard-boiled eggs,
and "It's hard, and it's hard, ain't it hard, great God,
        To love one that never will be true."
Because we have always lived
between a rock and a hard place.

Because of hard cider, hard knocks, hard times,
        hard luck, the Hardy Boys, Warren Harding,
and the "Hearty, Har, Har" of goofy cartoon laughter.

Because it's hard to tell, hard to believe, hard to fathom,
hard to recognize, hard to hold on,
hard to admit, hard to draw a straight line.

Because of hard living,
hard core
things hard to take,
things hard to hear,
things hard to admit.

Because you barely get there when you have to go back.
Because you hardly get settled when you have to move on.

Because "It's a hard, and it's a-hard, it's a-hard,
                                and it's a hard
        And it's a hard rain's a-gonna fall."

Because of hard and fast rules, hard tack,
hard knocks in the middle of the night,
hardening arteries,
hard places to get to, hard lines to cross,
hard decisions to make.

Because, sometimes, everyone's hard as nails

and it's hard to be upright, and it's hard to bear witness
and it's hard to see your way clear
and it's hard to stay clean and it's hard to stay sober
and it's hard to love and it's hard to beat the odds,
and it's hard to untangle yourself from politics and
    fishing nets
and it's hard to forgive, and harder still to be forgiven.

And "It's been a hard day's night, and I've been working
    like a dog.
        It's been a hard day's night, I should be sleeping
        like a log."

And because there are hard roads yet to travel,
hard truths yet to swallow,
and you must bite down hard or you'll scream.

hardware, hard wire, hard to please,
hard disk, hard copy, hard drive.

Because the Mohs scale doesn't begin to measure it
and the factory stood hard by the railroad yards.

"My eggs over hard, please."

Hard love, Hard Rock Candy Mountain, Hard Rock Café,
hard hats, hard facts, hardbacks,
hard steps to take, hard shoes to fill,
take a long hard look,
the bigger they are, the harder they fall.

Because iron is hard, and steel, and granite and marble.
Because of hard sauce poured over plum pudding.

Because it's hard to explain
Gibraltar, St. Peter, the anchor,

hard liquor, hard landing, hard pressed,
hard labor, hit hard, hard stop,

this shadowy place,
these difficult, arduous days.

The Book Lovers of Round Lake

Insomnia, most said. What other reason
would cause the women of our town
to stay up reading until almost dawn?

Fully dressed, their curtains never drawn,
they sat by picture windows, reading on and on,
snowfall to windblow, books in golden cones

of light upon the laps of Mrs. Brown,
and Mrs. O'Brian, Mrs. Sheilberg, old Miss Stone—
the teacher who never married Mr. Silverton.

Mysteries? Romance? No child crossed their lawns
to sneak up close enough to look upon
what they were reading. And now they're gone

well into the night. The August moon,
fireflies and will-o-the-wisp, and you, bookbound
author, love them as you would your own.

Sleepy Old Towns

In America, we have them, too—old towns
huddled under forests,
or alongside the kind of rivers that always seem to
     flow calmly
into the west.

Here are the antique shoppes, the oak lane walks, the
     lullabyes,
the slow falling snows,
and cellars and attics and antebellum porches and the
     tinny sound
of old radios.

Towns that never flourished, towns where everything
lingers too long,
where moss grows under the shutters of dilapidated houses,
and no one seems young.

Rip Van Winkle towns. Winesburg, Ohio. Poker Flats.
Hannibal, Missouri.
The heartbreak town of Grover's Corners and the
     dog-eared one
of Yellow Sky.

And out on the river, the mist,
and deep in the forest, the devil;
where the world's just an eagle's wing in the dusk, or
     a cloud,
or the moon growing pale.

The devil entices the good man
who ventures too far.
The river's too dark. You'll lose your way, you'll drown in it
even under the stars.

Morning town, Frenchmen's Bend, Lonesome Dove,
Gopher Prairie,
Eatonville, Cooperstown, Old Eben Flood lying
    drunk on the hill
over Tilsbury.

Stepping on Shadows

When I first heard it was impossible
for the foot that made it to step on its own shadow,
all one summer I tried to do it anyway,
watching my shadow grow

from nothing at noon
to more than twice its proper length as evening came
down upon the streets of my home town
when the evening train

rushed toward the mountains. Then,
if my shadow was behind me, I'd turn abruptly,
so it couldn't escape
and I'd literally leap

to knock it out of its shoes—but not once
did I succeed. Or, my back to the sun,
my shadow stretching ahead into some field or meadow,
I'd start to run

faster and faster. Yet my footsteps
never touched it at all.
I could only regard it balefully
as night fell

and my shadow reappeared
beneath streetlamps and in the light slivers
cast between narrowed curtains
that hid my future

and everyone else's. Still, how tempting,
how compelling for a while,
to be so certain I could place my own shadow
under my own self-control.

The Poet's House

"We almost rented it, you know,
    but it was so remote your father didn't know

if he could find work anywhere near.
    Still, we came very near

to renting it anyway. I liked the hilltop view,
    the apple tree in the yard. We held the view

then, that everything we did should be poetic
    one way or another. And how poetic

it would have been to sit at his window
    and watch the stars, and dream of a window

opening up for us—something so unusual
    happening to us we'd not live the usual

life most of us do. That we did. That he didn't:
    that poet of brooks and clearings and deer that didn't

run when you approached. We asked the price.
    It was a little too much, a price

we'd have had to borrow to afford and in the end
you were brought up in a walk-up end

New Hampshire apartment overlooking a street corner
as nondescript as the corner

of a three-cent stamp. Here, here's the poet's house
in this poem. I would have loved living in that house."

The House with Only the Sound
of a Dog Barking Inside

after a line from Haruki Murakami

On my morning paper route, I passed it every day,
the house with only the sound of a dog barking inside
out on the edge of our village—its curtains never parted,
its small porch always empty, nothing in the front yard
but yellow grass. From the tenor of its barking, the dog
was medium-sized, probably a mongrel, not really in distress,
but lonely, mildly afraid, needful of someone to hear him
and to somehow respond. . . . One summer, more or less
feeling sorry for the dog, I mock-barked back while I pedaled
my bicycle into, then out of its earshot. Yet since the house
wasn't a customer on my route, I never gave any more
than that minute or two of attention as I tossed
my papers onto adjacent porches and I never once
saw whoever fed and kept the dog inside that house.

I Was Eighteen

Arkansas, Missouri, Kansas, Nebraska—
        when I was eighteen I hitch-hiked across them,
trying to find out the truth about America.

I carried a sleeping bag, knapsack, film and a camera,
        pen and a notebook. I hitch-hiked in sunlight
    and storm
across Arkansas, Missouri, Kansas, Nebraska,

Wyoming, Texas, New Mexico, Utah,
        and both Dakotas. I was eighteen. My dream
was to find out the truth about America,

whatever that was. Was she Utopia,
        "the last best hope of mankind"? Was she the same
across Arkansas, Missouri, Kansas, Nebraska

as she was in New England? I longed for great drama,
        some over-the-blacktop Hank Williams to come
and I would find out the truth about America.

But I was eighteen, naïve as clam chowder. Montana
was simply huge sky. Idaho, tubers. Nevada, a game.
        And in Arkansas, Missouri, Kansas, Nebraska,
they just smiled when I asked them the truth about
        America.

Elvis

I

Your name an anagram for "evils" and for "lives,"
of course we followed you. I wore
blue suede shoes, long sideburns, turquoise shirts,
and tried to learn guitar,
but the best that I could do was play "Heartbreak Hotel"
on my harmonica. . . . You were

what our parents tried to chase away,
moonshine, warble, A-bomb, drive-in sex,
so raw and aw shucks innocent at once
girls never knew which Elvis would come next,
the bedroom eyes,
or country boy up to his country tricks.

II

Late in '56, a knowing teen could drive
three hundred miles
from Elvis song to Elvis song, one picking up
where the other faded into needle clicks. Silvered dials
spun through endless stations playing faint or loud
your "Hound Dog," "Love Me Tender," "Don't Be Cruel"

into my high school junior and my high school senior
    year.
You were our troubadour before I knew the word,
black voice coming out of white,

English honeyed, jazzed up, sultry, blurred,
then pure alto clear. You made Perry Como sound
like oatmeal curd.

Self-creating, self-destructing, petulant,
rocking from the flip side of the tracks each night,
you were the rebel girls could form by proper love,
another wrong America turned right.
If you could swing yourself from Memphis, then
any smart-assed boy could see his name in lights.

III

When I finally left you, Elvis, it was for
college books, for coeds who hummed Bach, for poetry
by Ginsberg, Corso, Kerouac. . . .
Strange fruit hanging from a Southern tree
grew into civil rights and Ban the Bomb
and finally into Vietnam. These weren't your urgencies.

Yet you still sang on. Down through the years, Teddy
    Bear,
I caught you here and there
strumming underneath our new hypocrisies,
your raunchy brashness curled in gospel prayer.
The audience was screaming as you took the stage,
"Elvis! Elvis! Elvis!"—king of comeback, heartthrob of
    despair.

Winter Semester

(Syracuse, 1959)

My room was the size of two large closets,
and held a dresser, a single bed against
a plain beige wall. Its one window faced
the cracked slate shingles of roof cornices
and I could only make its yellow shade
stay all the way up or down. Cross-legged,
I typed on the floor, my back held straight
by a carton of books. Each Sunday, I bought
a box of saltine crackers and a quart of milk
then sogged them in the plastic cup I'd lick
clean as a begging bowl. Eyes had struck me dumb,
Alan Watts' eyes, how everything had come
into place when he addressed the Hall of Languages
clad in black robes, breathing Zen—the ridge
of one eyebrow lifted like a miniature windowsill
over our planet. And so I tried to fill
my head with nothing but bright emptiness
and lack of desire. Evenings, I practiced
breathing and silence, staring at the snow
falling on the cornices below,
or I straightened the room again, again, until it had
nothing but pure lines of my perfectly made bed,
closed drawers, the dustless dresser top,
upright spines of all the books I'd stopped
desperately reading. For three months I spoke
only in monosyllables. Often, I took
long walks to nowhere but a grove of pines

in Thornden Park, or down the Eire railroad line
until the university became a Taoist dream
and a drumlin of moonlight. It seemed
as if I was disappearing, as if the world
was disappearing—as if . . . if I called
my name out it would also disappear
into weather and stars. I remember
how, with a few decisions, I could set aside
my wants so only basic needs remained—
food, clothing, shelter—my life so simplified
that each new happening was like a vivid blade
of new sedgegrass sprung up among the old.
I fell and fell into each different spell,
through focus, through pastel hues. Hendricks Chapel
bells would peal class hours and, alone,
dazed in my tiny room, within their sound,
I could see a lotus blossom floating
under a bank of willows toward that spring
that took forever to come. Sometimes,
finding palmlines in the shade, lost fishing streams,
I knew that all which seems important
is only a flourished pattern of the thousand accidents
that bring us to the Now that never is
but only seems, approximates, and vanishes
as my meditations and my bare life did,
when warm rain streaked the window and the sad
accordion player in the room in back of mine
began to play "My Darling Clementine"
and "Red River Valley" and a polka
so sweetly, so longingly, I felt the "ah"
gasp in every note. Strange young voices lifted

on Comstock Avenue. Uncertainly, I drifted
back into their presence—one evening from the porch
I glimpsed two student nurses stretch,
discard white blouses in the house across the way.
Each day turned back into another day
or forward to the next. I'd lost every friend
as that semester closed yet at the end
of all eight but the last, the student
knows another Self can be laid out to fit
the next term opening. In April, I unpacked
my calendar and strewed my clothes, attacked
food like a wild man, thumbtacked movie posters
of *Spartacus* to the ceiling. In May, I wore
a suit and tie to finals. . . and it was over.
Other students would take what they could
of the life I'd tried and then abandoned
in that clean and barren room I've not
even driven past since—though who am I to forget
the cracks across its ceiling and my door
that opened on a hallway and five empty stairs
down to the second landing, ten more to the first
and then to the final door, a burst
of sub-zero wind—a wind where nothing living
could walk in upright or survive in very long.

Box Trucks

The first time I saw one toppled in a ditch, split open
like a huge empty Kleenex box ripped open,

lying on its side in rural Canada,
that year we'd taken to exploring Canada,

(ambulances gathered around it, their red lights flashing,
and it was late Winter, the Northern Lights flashing),

the first word that came to my mind was *flimsy*,
how unexpectedly thin and flimsy

its sheet metal sides. All those box trucks,
their heaviness, their huge substantiality, those trucks

like heavy lives continually bearing down upon us,
pulling out from behind us, cutting in before us,

were actually nothing more than flimsy rectangles,
used as containers. No wonder high winds blew these
     rectangles

when they carried only rope and cardboard, off the roads
and flipped them over, to lie beside roads

on hillsides like this one, almost as if panting. . . . The
    ambulances
nosed and backed and slid in mud until the last ambulances

left for Toronto, no sirens, flashing red lights turned off,
and then the police cruisers peeled off

into the Canadian dusk. Our stalled line of cars began
moving like beads unstringing, and after a while we began

to drive the box truck from our minds, along with all
our thinking we should be concerned with anything
        more at all

than rain falling lightly, misting the pines — our voices
flimsy and lost, the rain sliding under our voices.

Ballade of the Protester

The peacesigns that we painted on the crest
of Sawyer's Mountain where huge boulders blur
into a three-state view, the raised clenched fist
we stenciled on the blank side of a granite spur
will be faded now—if they're even there.
It's been thirty years since we felt justified
imposing our convictions on the unaware,
our fists and peacesigns scattered nationwide.

Thirty years. . . . We climbed through rag-tailed mist
and rain so soft you called it sweet liqueur,
singing Joan Baez and Arlo Guthrie, Jimi Hendrix,
country Joe McDonald and Joe Crocker.
Out to change the world and stop the war,
self-righteous in our sentiments and pride,
we tossed our symbols like our uncut hair,
our fists and peacesigns scattered nationwide.

But that's all done with now. We've placed a list
of fifty thousand names upon a wall of prayer
and turned away. Who would have ever guessed
the scale we tipped would topple in the air

and when uprighted would be even more unfair?
New histories darken those who took our side.
Though. . . thirty years ago. . . we hitch-hiked everywhere,
our fists and peacesigns scattered nationwide.

Ballade, I make you for the days we wore
thick black armbands, for the halls we occupied,
for Woodstock, Washington, Kent State–our lives cocksure,
our fists and peacesigns scattered nationwide.

Because a Blue Heron Flew Overhead

Because a blue heron flew overhead,
it was a good day to butter bread,

to listen to James Taylor, *Stockbridge to Boston*,
and visit the Garden of the Unsuccessful Politician.

A good day to ask a clock what makes it tick,
or place one brick upon another brick,

to remember that if you think, there are ripples,
but also if you don't think, there are ripples.

And because a blue heron flew overhead,
we swept up the porch, we made up the bed.

We bought packaged shirts, then took out their pins.
We placed gray umbrellas in clear storage bins.

There was a road, a lake, a moonlit field,
a brow to be soothed, a wound to be healed.

Stockbridge to Boston. *Sweet Baby James*.
The glory, the wonder, the sheer joy of names!

And my life was a story of thread and unthread
because a blue heron flew overhead.

II

Other Fish in the Sea

for Sarah B.

Just as I predicted—that boulder's shadow
was really a Wild discus,
and if you approach that shoal a zebra starfish
might make you laugh.

There's a torpedoray, and there
a Sailfish sculpin,
a Sapphire devil off to the right. Veer, turn,
keep your eyes open,

and you might come upon the most
handsome flameangel, or a Lions cove yellow labido
who's spent a lifetime waiting
only for you

as you swim this vast sea. Look,
there's a black perch, a headstander,
a Red Irish Lord, a yellowtang,
a Jordan's snapper,

all those others
you kept your eyes from
in this wave-tossing love and adventure
you now resume,

and even more wondrous—see,
off in the coral,
Azure damsels, a thousand soles, the black and yellow sail
of a wild Moorish idol.

Joe's Song

In the old pool hall in Mechanicville,
      under the dunce-cap lights,
we shot a few, and then a few more few,
      killing the nights

until, beer foaming our brains,
      we wove to the door.
I think we thought not a lot
      about being poor.

Where the streets of Mechanicville met
      in a cluster of shops,
under the green-striped awnings,
      we taunted the cops,

and mocked the over-dressed dummies
      (Emily, Russ).
With the hard-pupil eyes of the wealthy,
      they ignored us.

They ignored us. The wealthy
      don't blink a lash;
poor, white, disgusting, they call us:
      poor white trash.

But, by Jesus, they'll never know, never,
      our blown appetites,
how laughter runs rings around laughter,
      Mechanicville nights,

when a push to the shoulder means
        a man is a friend
and he'll joke you to Death, and beyond it,
        arise or descend.

Lazarus, rich men call
        from their flameholes of dung,
dip the tip of your finger in water
        and soothe my scorched tongue,

the priest said last Sunday. I don't
        know if Father was right,
but if I was Lazarus . . . well,
        on Mechanicville nights

who ponders such things? Life's crazy,
        a dried wishbone chance.
The moon is a numskull. Yet Loretta,
        how she can dance!

Buddha's Hand

(Citrus medica var. digitata)

The lemony scent of it
      pervades this room.
Its gnarled, arthritic fingers,
      curled, presume

our prayers to come. Curious,
      we examine it closely,
the canary-yellow rind,
      the almost grotesque way

its fingers cluster
      each into each:
octopus tentacles,
      mutated starfish,

and think it not at all
      the earth-touching hand
of the Buddha at the moment
      he was enlightened.

Out of the Blue

Lion, tyger, panther, figured wheel,
       the carriage, *La Belle Dame sans Merci*,
small rain, hunted hare, ball-turret gunner,
       flea on a bonnet, witness tree,

starry night, Daddy, groundhog, Grecian urn,
       west wind, my cat Geoffrey,
hurt hawk, pool player, Thomas the Rhymer,
       coy mistress, jar in Tennessee—

they all come out of the blue, they spin,
       prance, whisper, wound, tease, run away,
settle for a moment, then are gone
       out of the mind and from this day—

Julia's clothes, country churchyard, darkling thrush,
       windhover, Lake Isle of Innisfree,
Musee des Beau Arts, earth's imagined corners,
       red wheelbarrow, papa waltzing, Annabell Lee,

daffodils, London snows, a noiseless patient spider,
       trout on a hook, three ravens, Apeneck Sweeney,
proud music, cuckoo song, the Metro station,
       Jenny's kiss, chambered nautilus . . . this light
         blue elegy.

Do You Know the Muffin Man?

Do you know the Muffin Man,
The Muffin Man, the Muffin Man?
Do you know the Muffin Man
Who lives on Drury Lane?
                    —Child's Nursery Rhyme

Yes, actually, it so happens
I *do* know the Muffin Man.
He's a broad-faced, pleasant fellow
who lives on Drury Lane.

I like his oatmeal muffins,
his blueberry muffins, his bran,
the banana-nut muffins he bakes
in his shop on Drury Lane.

I like how happy he is,
how he tells jokes in the rain
when he hands us the muffins he brings
from his shop on Drury Lane.

There's a sort of Zen to him,
like loss rerouted to gain,
a calmness, a look in the eyes
that may come from Drury Lane.

But it also may have to do
with the muffins themselves, the muffins
to end all muffins, the ones
you might find on Drury Lane.

The ultimate muffins, the muffins
to die for, the muffins of fame,
the gray goose muffins, the cusp
of the muffins of Drury Lane,

the muffins of Meaning, the muffins
none can explain,
the smell of the muffins, the taste
of the muffins from Drury Lane.

So *"Muffins! More muffins!"* we shout
at the sight of the Muffin Man
and the cart he wheels each morning
filled with muffins from Drury Lane.

And the muffins are warm and sweet
as they crumble in our hands,
each baked by the Muffin Man
who lives on Drury Lane.

The Beginner

Because he's read about it in a book on Zen
and there were lilies-of-the-valley on the table
in a thin white vase, he took the morning
to look at them and only them, to concentrate
all his attention on the lilies-of-the-valley.

Sick of politics, society, and war, he wanted only Zen
answers to the universe. Where but a kitchen table
could be a better place to start? Where but a morning
splashed with paradoxes and absurdities? Concentrate.
There's nothing in the world but lilies-of-the-valley.

Each bell-blossom on the stem is Zen,
he thought, and the three that fell upon the table,
also Zen—as is this entire morning,
the way the seconds and the minutes concentrate
and separate, like lilies-of-the-valley.

Puns flashed across his mind: Now and Zen,
Zen Commandments. Mice and Zen. Elbows on the table,
head in hands, he scarcely moved all morning,
images distilled, dissolving like a concentrate,
eyes focused solely on the lilies-of-the-valley.

Suspended in its bubble made of Zen
the sun cast flower-shadows on the table.
An old refrigerator hummed away the morning,
as if it, too, had vowed to concentrate
on being and not being lilies-of-the-valley.

And politics went on, and war, society, and Zen
kept leaping on and leaping off the table,
like a cat let loose will leap into the morning,
but then start stalking, focused, and will concentrate
on anything that moves among the lilies-of-the-valley.

"What is, I guess. I guess what's not is Zen,
perhaps," he whispered to himself. "There is a table
and there's not a table. Neither. Both." The April morning
kept on floating in Time's concentrate,
and lovely, lovely were the lilies-of-the-valley.

Turning Over a New Leaf

Few things seem easier. Holding the page or maple leaf
steady under your thumb, you slide your fingers
beneath its thinness, then lift, then flip it quickly
or let it reverse swan-dive like a swimmer
clowning around on a diving board. And there
you have it, a totally new side—veined strangely
or mottled, or carved with hieroglyphics,
perhaps even blank and shiny. The possibility
is anything can happen now: a single gust of wind,
a hurricane, one pen stroke or a whole book,
a whistle or a symphony. What lies ahead
demands there must be nothing you hold back,
the leaf deceptively light, the light revealing
almost at once what comes of such light turning.

The Folk Ballad of Neil Armstrong

When he was a boy, Neil Armstrong dreamed
        he was floating and couldn't land.
He skimmed, and he hovered, and he cried out loud,
        "Please, please let me understand!"

He lived in a house by a buckeye tree
        and rousted about in its deep dark shade.
He rode his bike down Ohio roads
        and fished in rivers where shadows fade.

But then he grew up and he took a ship
        all the way to the moon.
Buzz and Michael were there with him
        and Neil would be landing soon.

The moon looked dead as a ghost's pale face
        you might see in a haunted pool.
"Come," said the moon, "come down to me,
        if you are a fool, a fool."

"I'll come," said Neil, "I'll come to you,
        down to your cratered face.
I'll come or I'll die. I can't go back.
        I'm tired of living in space."

And Earth was a long, long ways away,
        a marble of white and blue
where clouds rolled on and oceans tossed
        and dreams came sometimes true.

The rockets roared and the numbers flared;
        Neil dropped to the moon's white lip.
"Go back," said the moon. "Go back, go back,
        You'll die in the crash of your ship."

"I ride the *Eagle*," Neil's voice sang.
        "I ride the *Eagle* to you."
Alarm bells rang and voices screamed,
        The dust cloud blew and blew.

"Houston, Houston, help me out.
        I miss the sea and sky.
If I can't find a place to land,
        I think that I will die."

The lights went on and the legs stood still.
        the engine arm went off.
A billion people wept and cheered
        upon the watching Earth.

And in his suit of white, Neil spoke
        the words you have in mind.
"That's one small step for man," he said,
        "a giant leap for mankind."

And Michael, in the mother ship,
        and Buzz who stood beside,
were silent as two fishermen
        who watch the rising tide.

Oh Earthmen, Earthmen, don't forget
        that once he walked up there,
and looking down on us, he thought,
        how beautiful and fair.

How beautiful the rolling clouds,
        how lovely to splash in the foam,
but lovelier still is the buckeye tree
        of my Ohio home.

Bronx Catholic

I saw a VCR, a stereo, and two computers
walk out of a truck. I saw the bony hands
of a woman with a habit stroke carnations
and a kitten burning on a two-by-four.
I saw Jesus. I saw Him at the newsstand.
He wore a robe of meadows and a plastic gun
was pointed at Him. I heard air-conditioners
crank and groan and drip. I saw Disneyland
on the morning news—or was it Washington
where cherry blossoms bloomed? I saw a mouth
opening and closing and a South Korean
at a Woolworth's counter selling fountain pens.
A basketball rolled by itself, pigeons flew south
over the Empire State. I heard Mary weep,
turn on her side and then go back to sleep.
How utterly amazing is the living proof.

Calvary

No further task than this. Dazed, he lifts
his head from his right shoulder.
Jerusalem, below him, is an underwater drift
of specks, flecks, swirling in the tidal blur

he descended through. Such a small
place, really: hovels, walls, dirt streets,
young women shawled,
lackluster soldiers sprawling at the temple gates. . . .

Eloi! Eloi! Vinegar and blood
swirl in his cry. The face that swims
before him is the face of childhood
running through olive groves, drinking from the brim

of a wooden barrel by a mountain stream. *Eloi!*
The cloth is rendered and the curtain split,
flesh destroyed,
candles in the temples lit

by fever-spotted hands. And now his eyes
close finally. Upon the hill of skulls
rain runs freely as a pack of lies
coursing the walls

of his father's house. . . . One night he woke
and saw a morning dove suspended in the air,
then felt an angel stammer in his throat,
"Love's the only issue of despair,"

turned on his side and slept, until the sound
of his mother sweeping, Joseph hammering
woke him again. And he rose to find
God's spring

had come into the world, and it was in
the lamb's soft gambol and the ass's bray.
Upon a wooden table set with wine,
the freshly broken bread and honey lay.

III

A Touch of Strange

Without it, a pepper shake of it at least,
the heron's sleepy look, the way green forests turn
almost silver in late summer afternoons
along the upper Hudson, and the twist

of lemon in a lovely woman's eyes — these
would not exist. Without it, no platypus,
no penguin gliding down a sheet of ice,
and no canoe-shaped clouds above moonrise.

The politician lacking it can stride across
a wooden stage, not hearing carpenters
who nailed these boards together ninety years
before his birth. Although he speaks to us

of war and homelessness, without a touch of strange
he offers one more series of straight lines;
no crows perch on his shoulders and no vines
twist his legs about. Lives cannot change

without a touch of strange, without the safe
falling from a perfectly blue sky,
the ancient smell of rot and hunters' cries
from mastodon tusks, the London waifs

still at play in Dickens, and the pebble-glass
a leaf dents when it floats into a pond
ruffled by the wind. What spins around
the normal compass is the wild morass,

its Merlin rocks and stones. We face the mysteries
each day, and turn away. And yet, what if
one morning, on an orange and gray clay cliff
at Martha's Vineyard, we find fleur-de-lis,

mandalas, thirteen stars and stripes, a stick
drawing of the President? Or hear Cat Stevens build
a tree hut out of song? Walk through a field
where meadowlarks and John Deere tractors speak

to one another. Then, you might understand
how strange it is to strangely be alive,
to put your current maps aside and dive
without a second thought from solid land

into the strangeness of Hokusai's churning sea,
Blake's marriage, Rilke's panther, Tichbourne's jail.
The real is always just a touch beyond the pale,
a needlepoint of fireflies in the Black Ash tree.

Prayer Flags

In that New England town with Buddhist undertones,
we come upon them lined along the public pier,
mainly white strips of cloth. But here and there
a blue or red one

fluttering among the rest. *Dry now, our tears,*
Let there never be another 9/11,
No more killing fields are written in smudged crayon,
or with ball point pen or magic marker

upon each flag. The off-shore breeze is strong.
It lifts up all, carrying these messages
into the ear of God. . . . "Let freedom ring,"
another says. Some whisper. Others beg

but no one will be cast aside, although
the Himalayas where God lives seem hugely far
from this small rocky harbor
with its Tibetans, Thais, Cambodians,

nets and lobster pots. . . . Above the wharf,
a clapboard restaurant sells three-for-fifty-cents,
fabrics from which flags are ripped. Incense
wafts over everything, a kind of surf,

when we sit down for lunch—noodle soup, almond
        paste—
and write our prayers in tiny Palmer script, and then
walk out on the public pier again
and bind them to a railing as the fishing boats drift past.

Political Styles

HIGH BEAMS

Everything's bright and fully lit—just dazzling,
except those coming at you can't see one damn thing.

LOW BEAMS

How safely downcast you round every curve.
You fear for us. We scorn your lost of nerve.

Tiananmen Square

Safe, in our democracies,
we watch the news:
The criminal breaks free,
the cop pursues.
Chinese students gather
in Tiananmen Square.

A new Venus probe
was launched last night.
We're digging up The Globe
but money's tight.
Thousands of faces stare
from Tiananmen Square.

Computer hackers spin
our lives around.
Magic Johnson's grin
seems world-renowned.
A torch ignites the air
in Tiananmen Square.

Two cans of catfood roll
across the screen.
Dogs done with digging holes
lick their chops clean.
The tanks move everywhere
in Tiananmen Square.

History grades are down,
newscasters say,
but the music's live uptown,
and it's a new day.
And it's a massacre
in Tiananmen Square.

In the gardens of Beijing,
stone fountains flow.
In hooded cages, crickets sing
to be let go.
Soldiers sweep pavements bare
in Tiananmen Square.

The global village draws
its claws in once again.
Camcorders turn their low-lux gaze
on other specimens.
Sorry. No more news from there,
from Tiananmen Square.

In This Time of Disbelief

The Tsunami Sonnets

I

"What is to be done?" wrote Tolstoi. "What
is to be done?"
They scrabble for rice, they lie
and die in the sun. . . . Help each one?
But the poor, they are always with us. They
multiply
unless starvation thins them. Then
feed them, and they multiply again.

"Don't spread yourself thin," said a priest.
"You must," said a brother
"do for each other
as you would have them do if they were you."
The poverty, the hoplessness, the pain!
Limit your life. At your limits, do what you can.

II

Bright morning and cold. Others, I suppose,
are out there piling up treasures,
getting from hour to hour
by work, or humor, or shared misery,
forgetting God. What luxury
to put Him in His place among the clouds,
release Him on Sundays:

elderly patient in a sailor's home.
I choose to deal with Him. He mutters and complains
about the flower beds, the shortwave set,
how I hold back my life. "Come," He says,
"care for my woes."
Into my port, baring His stinking cargo,
He steers His hardship of love.

III

Very well then, God, I concede
your all-knowing, my infinitesimal
knowledge of you. But what do I do now,
my search concluded at your cloudy wall?
Turn back? Turn back to what? Nothing compares
to these shifting veils of light, these contrapuntal
voices I now hear—or with the blurring
comfort I now feel.
Must I take up again what I've renounced?
You know my fear of bridges. It was hard enough
to cross them in the first place. Would you send me back
over the water on that narrow track?
Sure you would. Unless I'm marked by time,
you cannot free me from the world's quicklime.

IV

Sea-faring Lord—lord of the telescope,
sails and mast, the prow against the waves,
the distant island and the ringent grave,
deck and hold, net, harpoon, and rope,

grip my clasped hands clinging to the mizzen-top,
and with your storming make my sails concave,
heal the scourged back of the ocean-slave.
You round my life. You are my Cape of Good Hope.
And if my prayers to you are puny prayers,
the miserable heap of secrets only you dispel,
send colors to my ears, and to my eyes oblique
gull calls of Hell. Lord, it is you who stares
through the empty sockets of the turtle shell
and winds my soul and body with your marlinspike.

Quagmire

In it, we try to walk and talk
at the same time:
steps and words, steps and words
so undermined

nothing seems safe, no way seems out,
mud lies everywhere,
and the stink of the place, the shiftiness of it,
its murky air.

Do we crawl back? Do we muck on,
slosh to one side?
Left seems right and right seems left.
Nothing's verified.

Had we found clear rivers, we
could follow how they run;
had we talked the clouds apart
we could trail the sun.

But swamp and marsh and bog and fen
stretch all around.
The buzzard's on the crooked branch
and there's no high ground.

Pitfalls

How cleverly they're made, and even more
        cleverly hidden,
for although we've been warned about
        love and ambition,

these pitfalls still trap us. Just when
        it seems nothing can happen,
we fall, headfirst,
        right through the certain

into the uncertain. And just as now
        becomes now and then,
a walk through prime numbers turns
        irascibly Zen,

we'll find something concealed
        behind every new plan,
a secret design,
        some slight of hand,

so watch your step,
        distrust the too-plain,
glue your eyes to the ground,
        gainsay what you gain.

Ambition's pitfall
        is to not take a stand,
and the pitfall of Love
        is also quicksand.

In the Closed School, In the Occupied Country

"Suppose they gave a war and no one came,"
 the poster in our empty classroom read,
"who would fight tyranny in freedom's name?"

 The lectern was abandoned. Each chair looked the same
 as when we sat there, raised our hands, and said,
"Suppose they gave a war and no one came"

 while others nodded. Perhaps one felt ashamed,
 another outraged, another bowed his head,
 who would fight tyranny in freedom's name.

"If madmen stalk our cities, who's to blame?
 What innocent among you would forestall the dead?
 Suppose they gave a war and no one came,"

 the empty lectern whispered. "It's no game
 of liberty on platters, give us our daily bread.
 You must fight tyranny in freedom's name."

 The classroom snickered—nothing to acclaim,
 not even shelter from those bombers overhead.
 Unquenched, small evils set great worlds aflame.
 They gave a war. We talked. And no one came.

France

Surrealist of hedgerows, Baudelaire
of weeds blown low within a hunter's brake,
kite of sorrow in a small boy's frown,
and truffle scent beneath a winter lake,

how can I solve you? How can I begin
to push my breath out of your counterpane?
Who wrote the numbers on the widow's back
and tied my language to your liquid train?

Maze of computers, St. Joan of closed doors,
the skidding sound a thought makes in the dark,
red wine of the Internet, marshland of the Alps,
tunnel of grass that hides a meadowlark,

who placed those coffins in your bloodshot eyes,
planned your wedding through binoculars?
How does chamber music brokerage a wave?
Where's the chiffon in a calendar?

Marseilles of footsteps, Notre Dame of rot,
clipboard carrier of Vichy wounds,
miser who throws pennies in the Seine
because the Sorbonne stalks a waxing moon,

why do wrinkles form on solid glass
and wrack the skin your Monet freeways roam?
In Roland's name, I ask these things of you,
Great Mystery Grimace all my poems storm.

Teaching the Logical Fallacy

There's always something else you could have done:
said a sweeter goodbye,
packed a thousand brownies into her lunch,
worn that red vest.

Or you could have had the brakes fixed sooner,
you could have checked the television set for bruises.
On the road to Miami, you could have stopped
at the Mobil station, not the Texaco.

Studying harder wouldn't have been so bad.
You should have dated him, you should have married her.
If only you hadn't gone into that store
looking for kumquats, or was it tangerines?

There's always that missing thread, that kettle of fish,
the last cigarette before the final one,
a letter you should have insisted be done over,
the friend you shouldn't have dumped into the river.

Open wide. Smile for the camera. One more time.
You should have known she wouldn't call again.
That number was yours, that horse, that dog.
You might have got the flu shot when they said.

You should have followed that path into the valley.
Why did you wait? You should have killed that rat!
One hour a day, that's all it would have taken.
I told you so. You don't remember. Your fault.

There's always something more you could have whispered,
you should have learned your lesson from the wife of Lot.
Because you washed the car, it rained,
post hoc, ergo propter hoc.

Mare's Nest

By accident, we discovered it
> high in the mountains,
not far off the trail
> high in the mountains.

It wasn't what you'd expect,
> just brush and horsehair
woven clumsily together—
> just brush and horsehair.

It was empty, and yet
> somehow, we could tell
something had been curled there.
> Somehow, we could tell

whatever it was, it was
> not good news at all,
but bloody, a nest like that
> not good news at all,

for there was a stink, a stink
> of manure, a smell of hay
left by the trail—a stink
> of manure, a smell of hay,

of this we're certain. We're telling
> the truth as we saw it.
This is our truth, it's the truth,
> the truth as we saw it

high in the mountains,
        not far off the trail,
a mare's nest, God help us,
        not far off the trail.

Putting Legs on a Snake

We've been trying for hours to improve the snake,
       to make him walk like us.
Why slide? Why coil into a ball
       when he can walk like us?

Let the scales fall from you, Snake,
       and may your eyes close,
your tongue stop flickering.
       It isn't right the way your body flows.

We try to prop him up but he stays limp,
       squirming, undulating back and forth—
not like us, who run like pairs of scissors,
       hop like raindrops, stride a steady course.

Revise your color patterns, Snake,
       your one lung and your many vertebrae.
Learn to stroll down sunny avenues.
       How sinuous you look today!

But everything we put on him falls off
       and every time we turn around, he's gone—
slithered away to nothing, like a promise we once made
       without a single leg to stand upon.

The Cause

When you jump off a bandwagon, it rolls on
toward the cities' high places,
and you're left without music on an empty road,

nothing to guide you. Not even the moon
drenches each milepost. No joyous faces
when you jump off a bandwagon. It rolls on,

its pipers shrill, its drummers too loud,
yet you listen: thick notes, then thin traces
and you're left without music on an empty road.

Just you versus you—your pro, your con,
your rabbits in hats, your sleeves, your aces
when you jump off. A bandwagon? It rolls on.

Mobs crowd beneath church bells. Fireworks explode.
But you're not recalled. Clamor throbs in tight spaces
and you're left without music on an empty road.

There's not one startled whistle, not one flung baton,
no *At last, we've done it!*, no full scale embraces
when you jump off a bandwagon. It rolls on
and you're left without music on an empty road.

IV

Russet

Fall apples, browning apple cores,
the mottled carcass
of an old trolley car, abandoned
deep in the forest.

What was once ambitious,
robust, rambunctious,
now burned the ruddy
color of rust,

bourbon, monks' robes,
faith and trust,
the russet scrape against the skin
of reddish-brown cloth.

Triolet for Stephen Hawkings

At the Nth degree, where large is small
and small is large, and nothing's what it seems,
each passageway was once a wall
at the Nth degree, where large is small
and every whisper builds into a call,
a black hole is a white hole is a dream
at the Nth degree, where large is small
and small is large, and Nothing's what it seems.

At 65

I

Don't stare at the sun. And yet I do, until
I leave it lying on the distant hill
three panes above my Study's windowsill,

then close my eyes to see its image burn
in deepest space: a blazing nub of corn
sown in dark soil, one gold button torn

from a king's lapel—then open them to stare
at a blank white wall, and there
it is a black hole scorched in purest prayer.

II

At least that's how a mystic might interpret such
transformations of the ordinary, clutch
at straws because the Far's too far to reach

unless the mind's vast bag of tricks
is slightly ruptured and the mind's eye flicks
upon what has escaped: the crucifix,

twigs of the bodhi tree, the lotus bloom,
smokewaves drifting to that farthest room
where all's transfixed in crystallizing foam.

III

I, on the other hand, the hand without
the mustard seed or Alexander's knot,
wait patiently, blink rapidly, until the spot

breaks into tiny asteroids, the last mote glows
and scattering to ash mixed into snows,
finally disappears. It's apropos

of how a scientist sets final things aside
to clear his desk of all the starry-eyed
solutions he cannot prove bonafide.

IV

The gray cat hotsteps on the heater grate,
my oval smoke rings twist to figure-eights,
I unbend paperclips until they're nearly straight

and line them in the *ch'ien-ch'ien* hexagram,
but my imagined power soon turns sham,
a breath that's forced up from the diaphragm,

so I stare out again. But now the sun
is just a buzz of light, a blur, a stain,
a decal sliding to the lower plain.

V

I stroke the cat, crush out my cigarette,
lift one hand idly to a Maine-bound jet,
wind up a music box and watch the pirouette

of its ivory dancers in their wigs and frocks.
I note the time on disagreeing clocks.
The castle that I'm building from my stumbling blocks

waits almost finished on the darkened floor.
Above the staircase dropping to death's-door,
I'll place a pewter wizard and a sunblind minotaur.

The Watershed

for Lori

From here
everything drains away,
our children
far down the rapids;
our parents,
mist faces.
Thirty years
up from lowlands;
through birch and pine,
aspen, poplars,
hand over hand,
we've climbed
to this
shadowy place:
forest stumps,
dried tussock marsh,
one sparrow
honed in the air.
Now we wait
for whatever happens,
taking our measure
from God knows where
or the dreamy whir
of dragonfly wings,
the chameleon guise
of water
seeping downhill

through the erratics,
ferns, club mosses,
scouring rush.
In dusk, not dark
we explore
what little is left
of ourselves,
what more
we must give,
who were once
irresponsible strangers,
out on the pond,
blowing our breath
at leaf boats,
whirligig beetles.

Quantum Physicists in a Night Garden

Time can be extinguished like a blown-out flame.
Black holes dissipate to God knows where,
　　yet everything we've said and done remains

　　like these lilies floating in this garden pool. Each name
we've said, each paper lantern strung, each cross we'll bear
　　in Time can be extinguished like a blown-out flame

yet floats forever here. It's paradoxical. All loss is gain.
We think we're still the people that we always were
　　since everything we've said and done remains,

　　but all is spin and sparkle, wave and particle. "What came
before? What happens next?" we ask. What currents stir
　　when time has been extinguished like a blown-out flame,

　　dwarf lilies float dark randomness? If Physics is a vein
of order/chaos, chaos/order, likewise it's a mirror
　　of everything we've said and done. Nothing can remain

　　beside this garden pool of scattered rain
and rising mist, and yet it does. What flowers here! We swear
　　everything we've said and done remains,
　　but Time can be extinguished like a blown-out flame.

Wild Oats

Slender, Short, Common, Moroccan,
  Western, Downy, Meadow, Poverty,
Winter—how many
  wild oats I've sown

over the seasons, Montana to Maine,
  Missouri to Kansas,
Iowa, Texas,
  sowing my grain.

Yet how little has grown,
  how little remains
on mountains and plains
  of the wild oats I've sown.

Sudden Death

after John O'Donahue

Where does the flame go,
the wave disappear,
eyes, breath, touch,
all gone at once,
dreams, thoughts, Eros,
swept away,
the memory of numbers,
fingers in wet clay;
sorrow, doubt, shame,
laughter, clinging, spite,
windows blazed with morning,
streetlights in the night,
the here that is not here,
taken in one stroke,
leaving us with dust,
Detroit,
Atlantic Beach,
burnt wick,
and candle smoke.

Cloud No Bigger than a Man's Hand

It approaches from the sea, too small
for thunder and lightning
but ominous as a closed fist
and what it will bring

nearing us, growing larger,
is completely unknown.
Beware the leaves blowing, beware
the spot on the sun.

All is turned toward it. It rides
the brow of the mind.
Soon, it will shadow one cliff
and a small lifeguard stand.

Beware the leaves blowing, beware
the spot on the sun.
Do your work well. Behold
the work yet to be done.

Solace

Newtown, CT

There are the fields we'll walk across
In the snow lightly falling.
　　　In the snow lightly falling,
There are the fields we'll walk across.

There are the houses we'll walk toward
In the snow lightly falling.
　　　In the snow lightly falling,
There are the houses we'll walk toward.

There are the faces we once kissed
In the snow lightly falling.
　　　In the snow lightly falling,
There are the faces we once kissed.

Incredible how we laughed and cried
In the snow lightly falling.
　　　In the snow lightly falling,
Incredible how we laughed and cried.

Incredible how we'll meet again
In the snow lightly falling.
　　　In the snow lightly falling,
Incredible how we'll meet again.

No small hand will go unheld
In the snow lightly falling.
        In the snow lightly falling,
No small hand will go unheld.

No voice once heard is ever lost
In the snow lightly falling.
        In the snow lightly falling,
No voice once heard is ever lost.

                    December 2012